PRINTED BY
PRINTER INDUSTRIA GRAFICA SA. PROVENZA 388 BARCELONA
SANT VICENÇ DELS HORTS 1985
D.L.B.: 17216-1985

CLAIRE BRETECHER

mothers

TRANSLATED FROM THE FRENCH
BY ANGELA MASON AND PAT FOGARTY

METHUEN · LONDON

7

SPRING EVENING

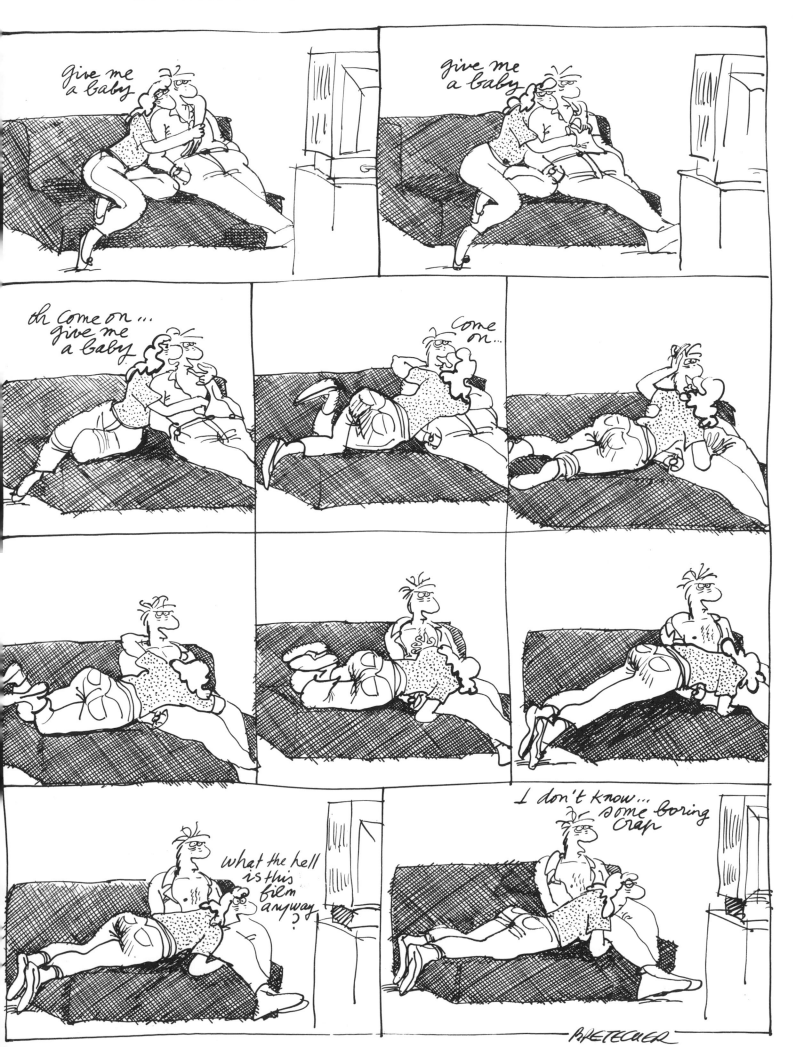

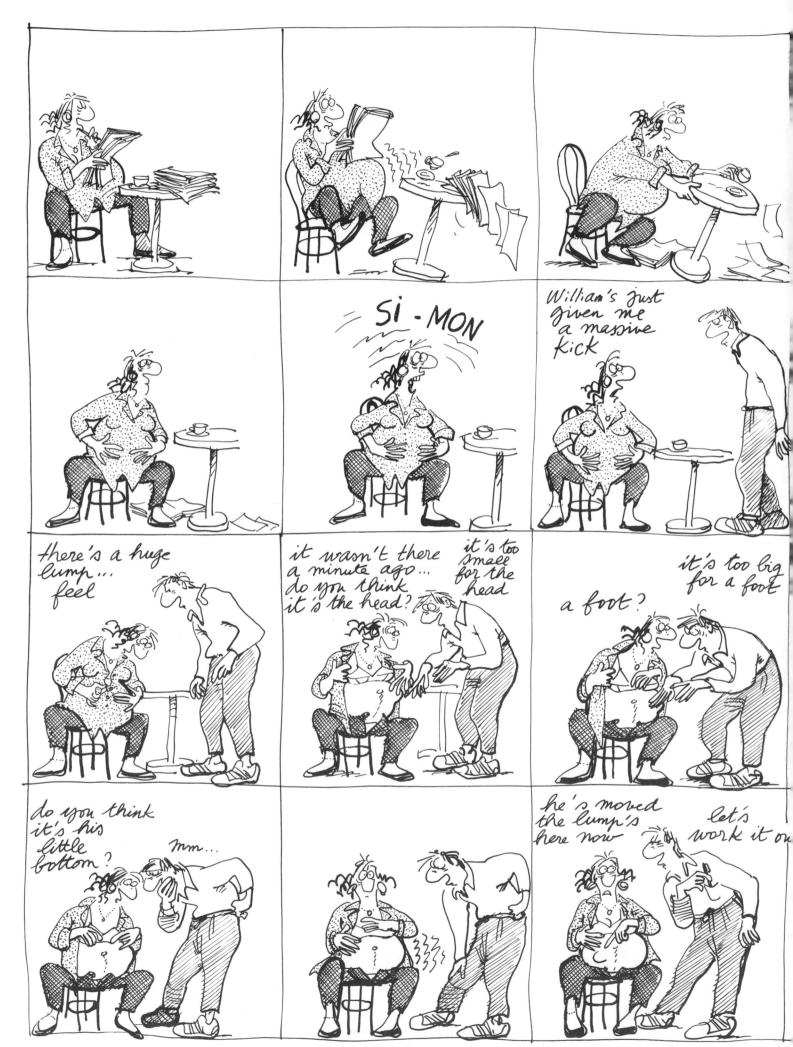

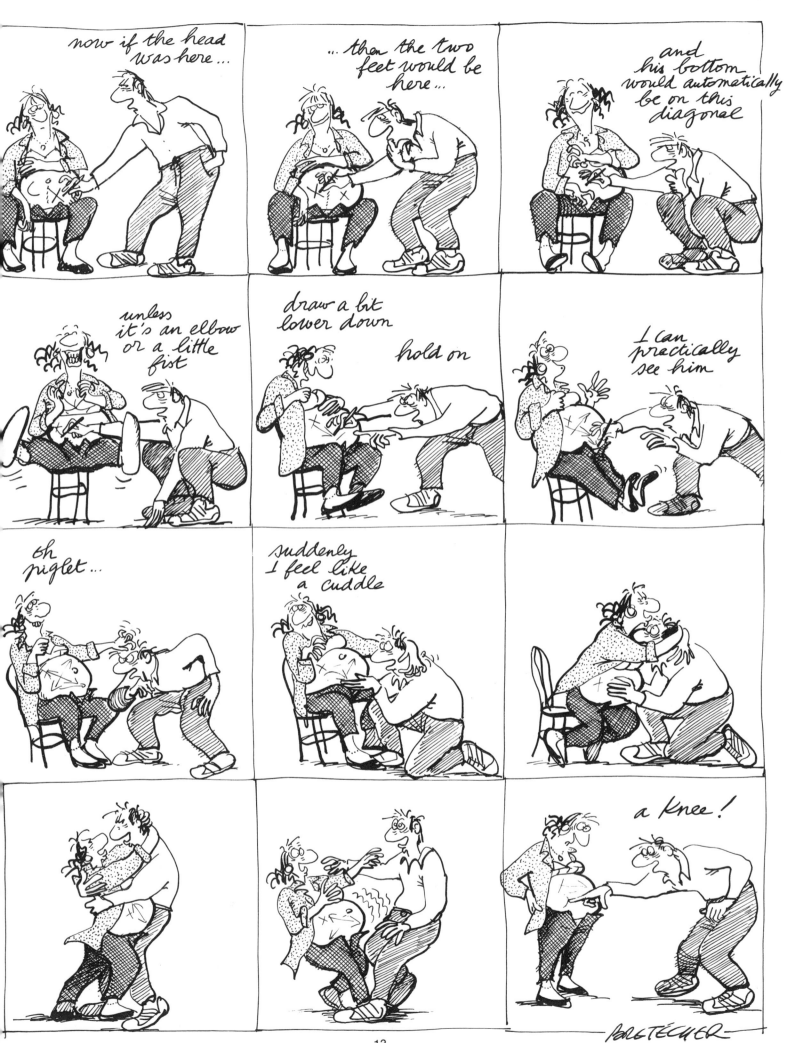

13

FATTY

GEORGE AND FELIX

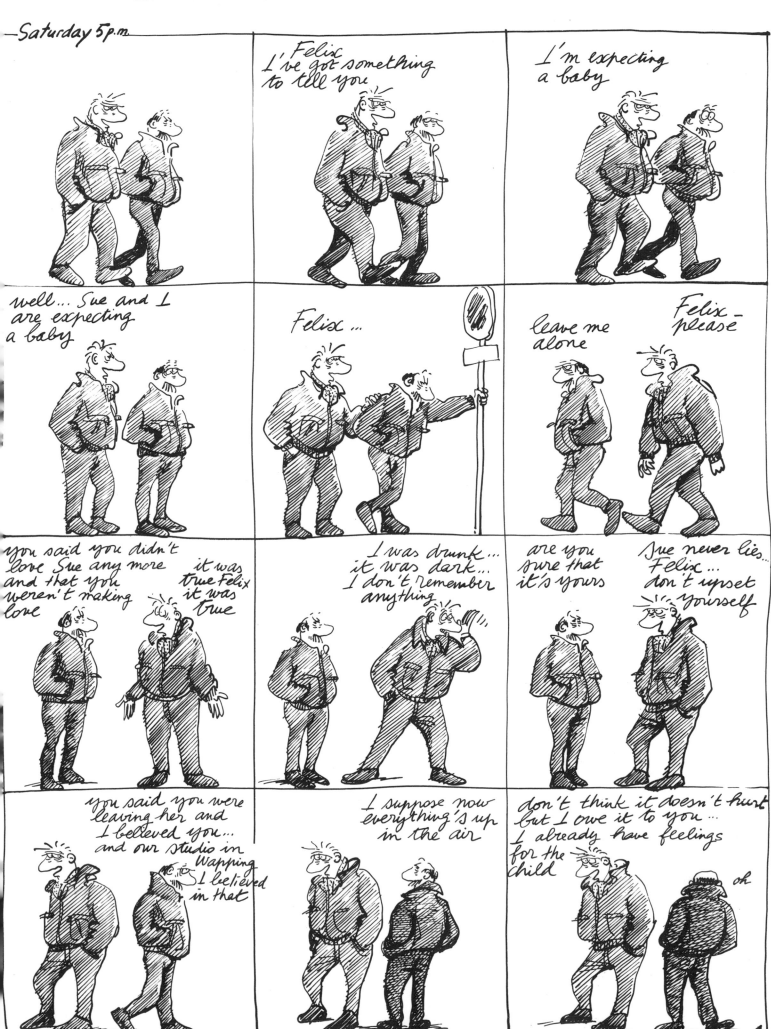

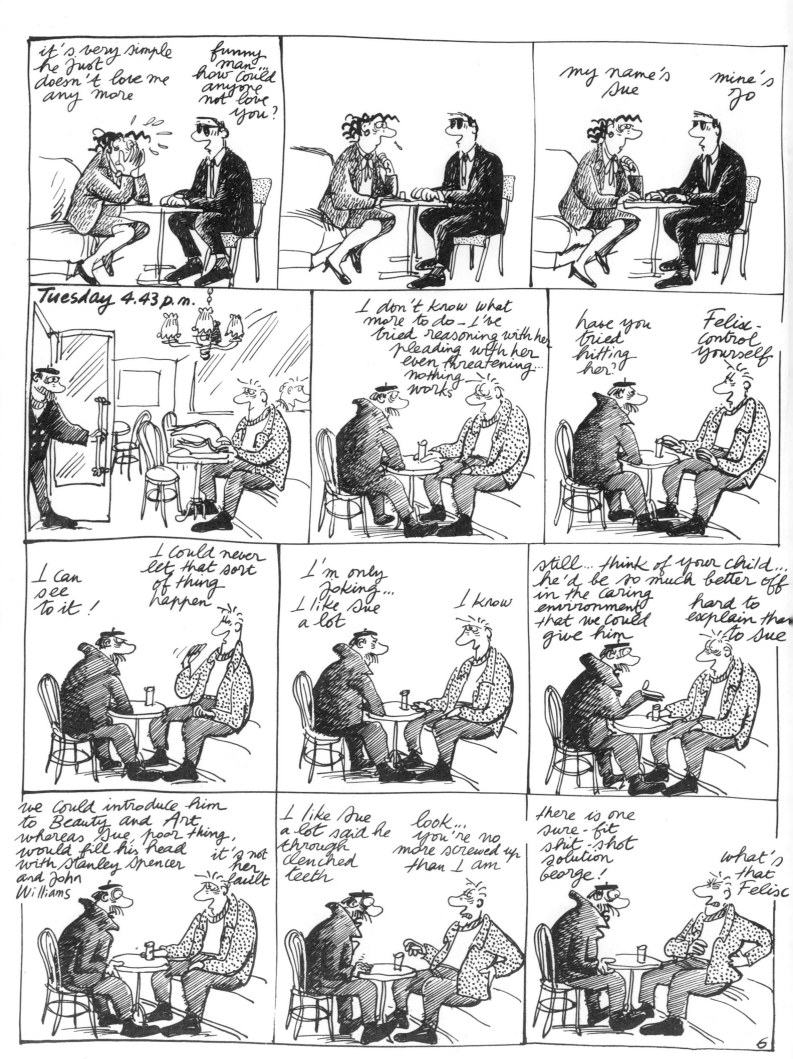

22

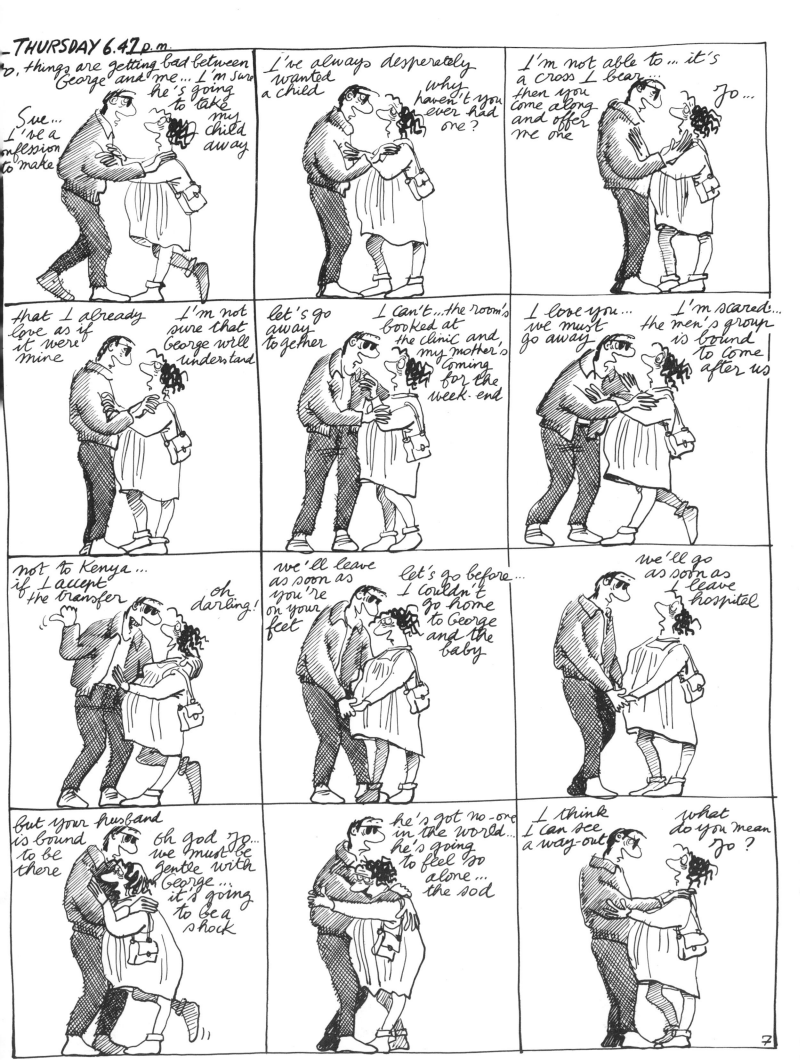

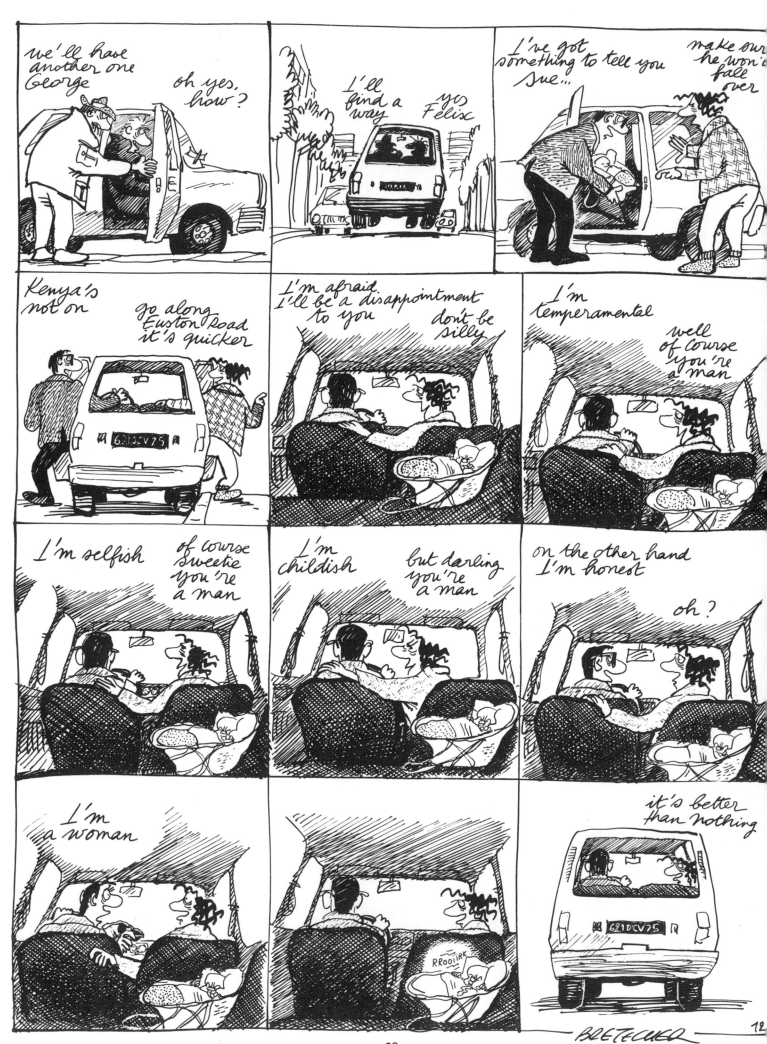

28

REJECTED

BARBARA

I was the first one in my class to lose it ... the first to get a divorce everyone called me a whore

at 20 I had my first real assigment, Crossing Ethiopia on a camel

everyone said it was very unfeminine

I spent two years at UCLA, three years in Peking, crossing Manchuria on a bike and they said it was irresponsible

after her third my sister got into feminist pottery and everyone said our mother should be proud of her

when I did my one woman sex show at the Whitechapel they told me I should get myself seen by R.D. Laing

I started my computer company and they all said I was into power

If I picked a baby up everyone said I wanted one

if I didn't pick it up they said I was embittered

so to get my own back I decided to have one with Luke, my niece's eldest son

YIPPEEE

in three months no-one can get me

BREZECLUER

ANGEL

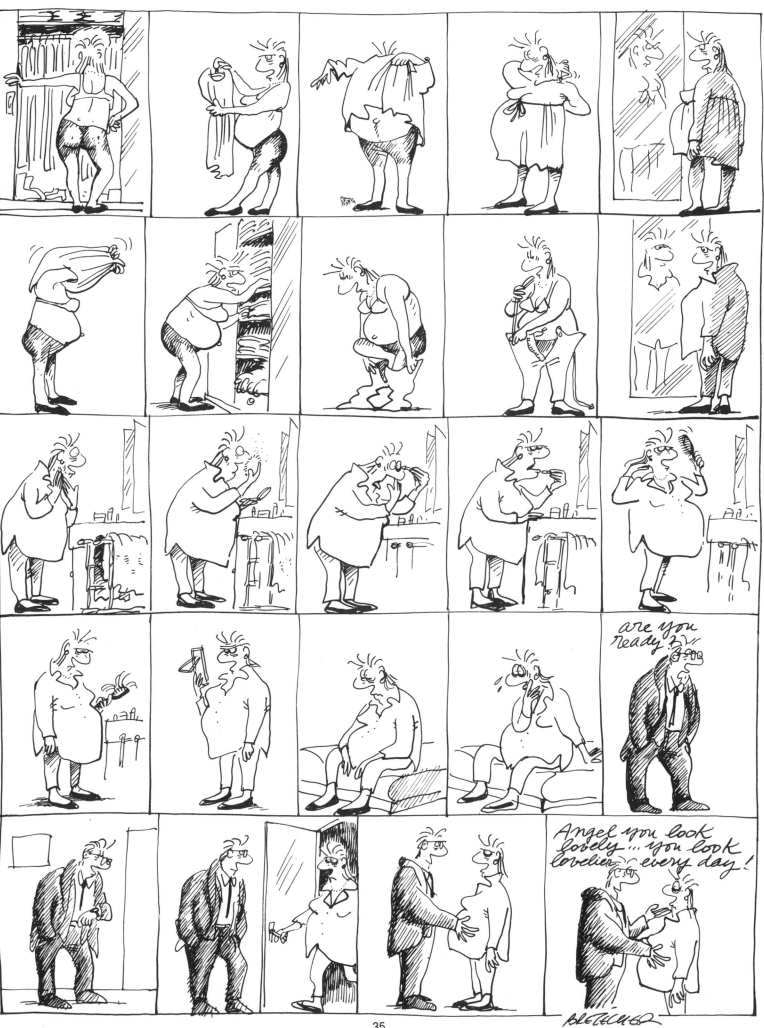

are you ready?

Angel you look lovely ... you look lovelier every day!

35

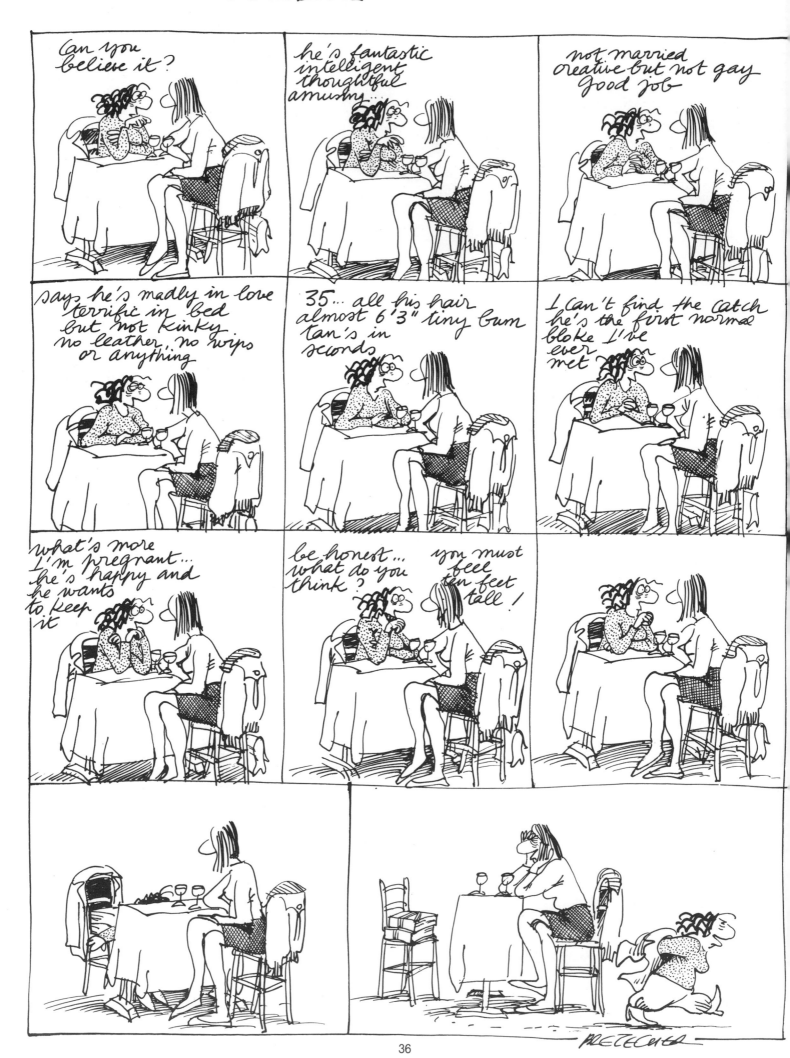

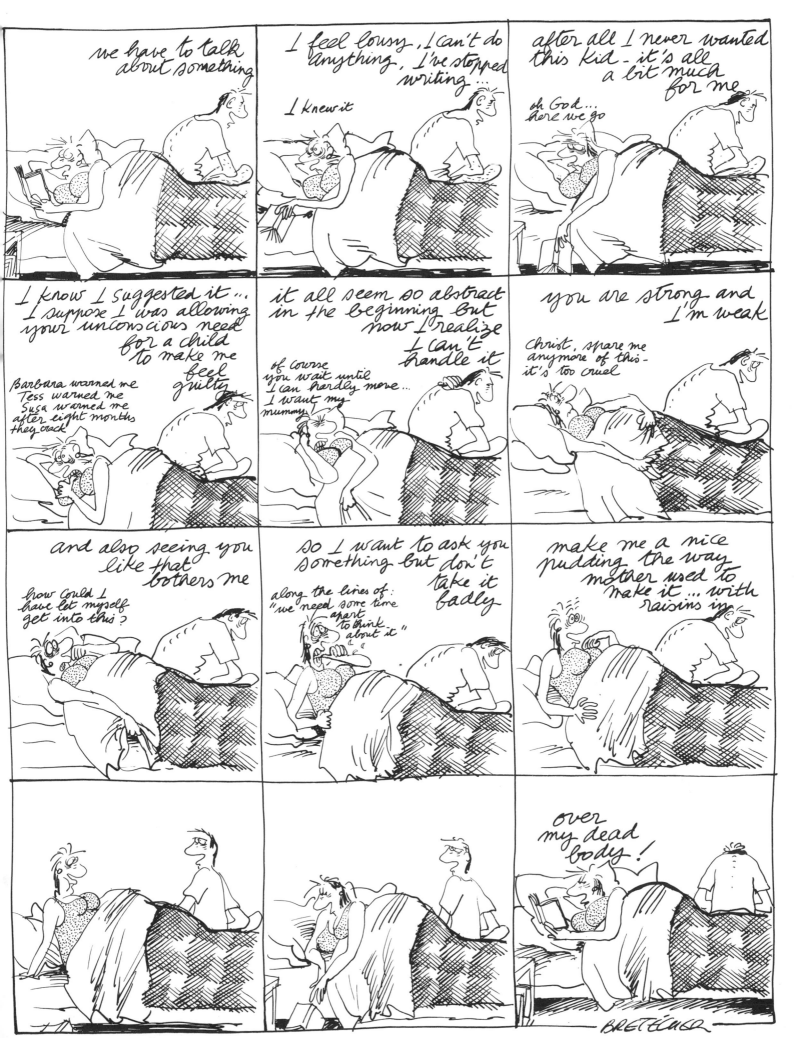

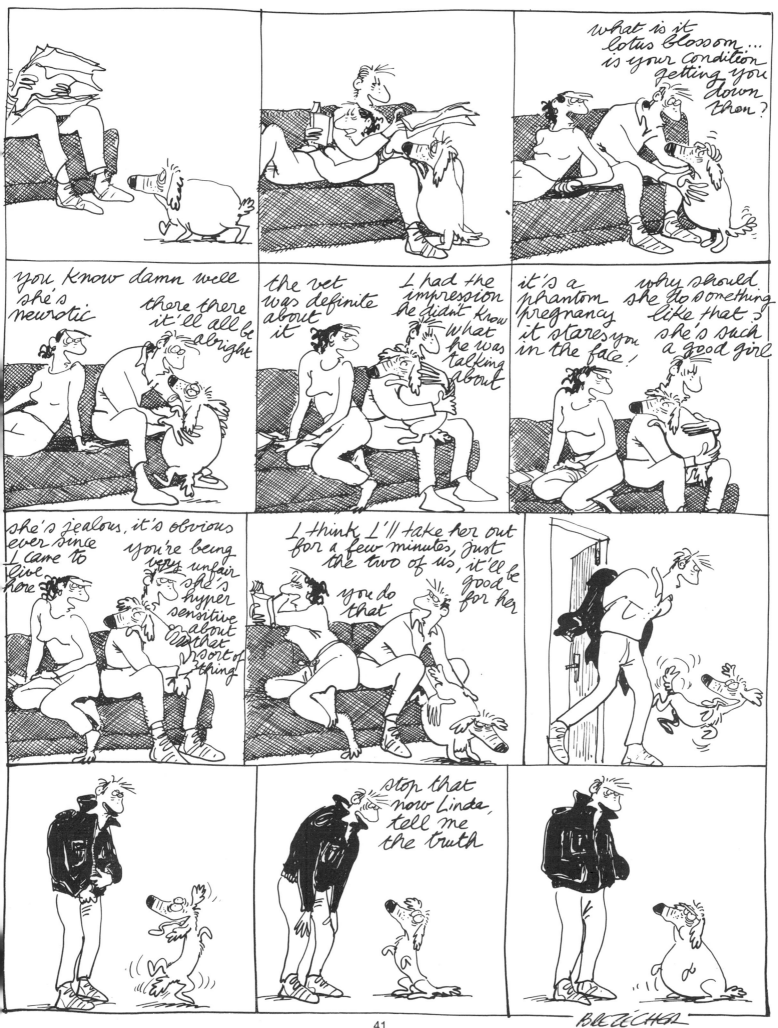

THE SLAVE

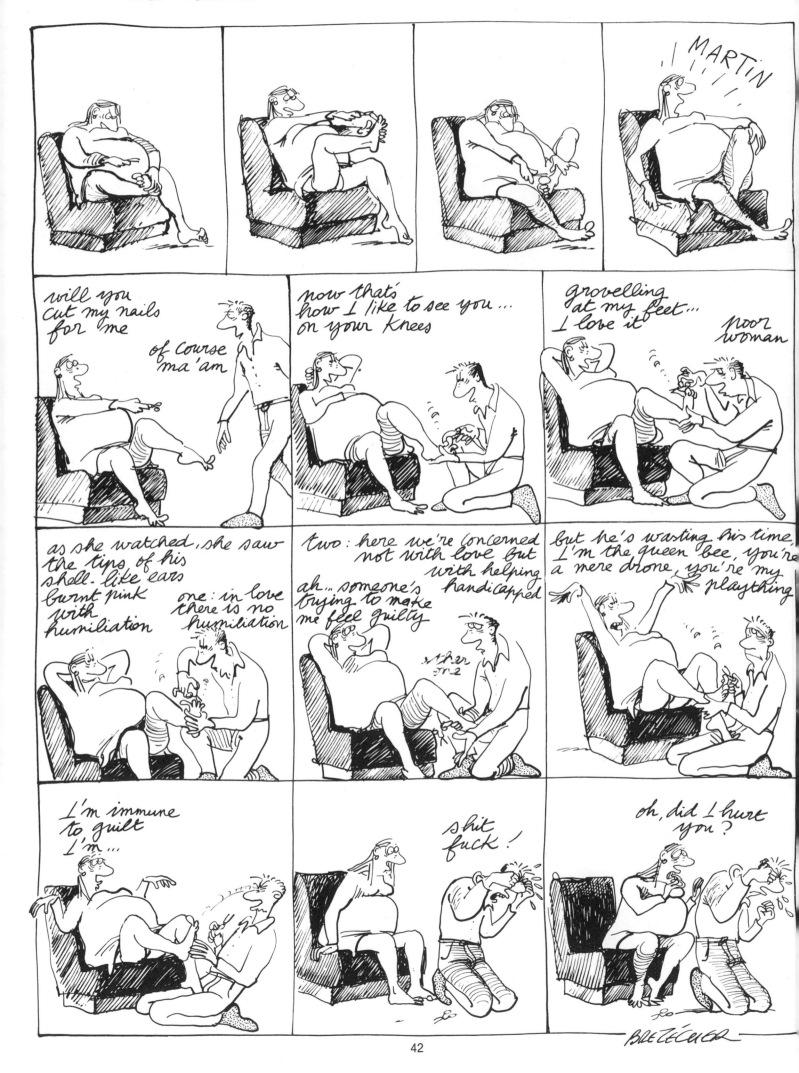

THE CLAIRVOYANTES

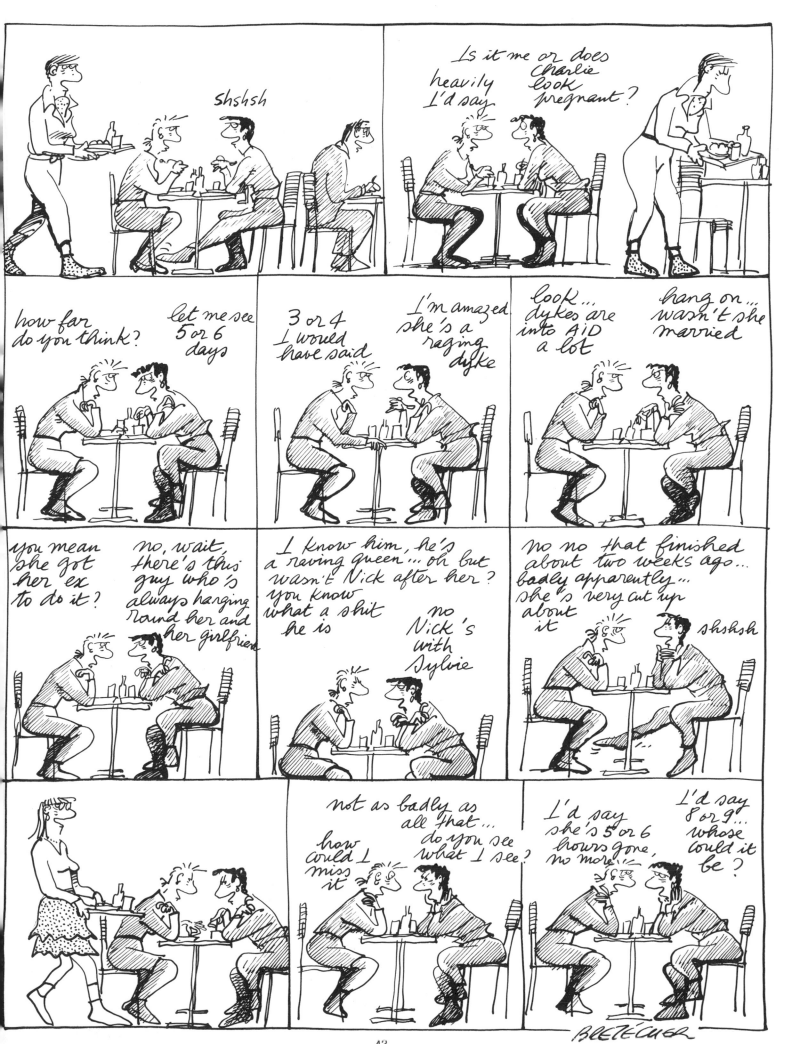

Sophie

PINK BOOTEES

BRÉTÉCHER

PLAYMATE

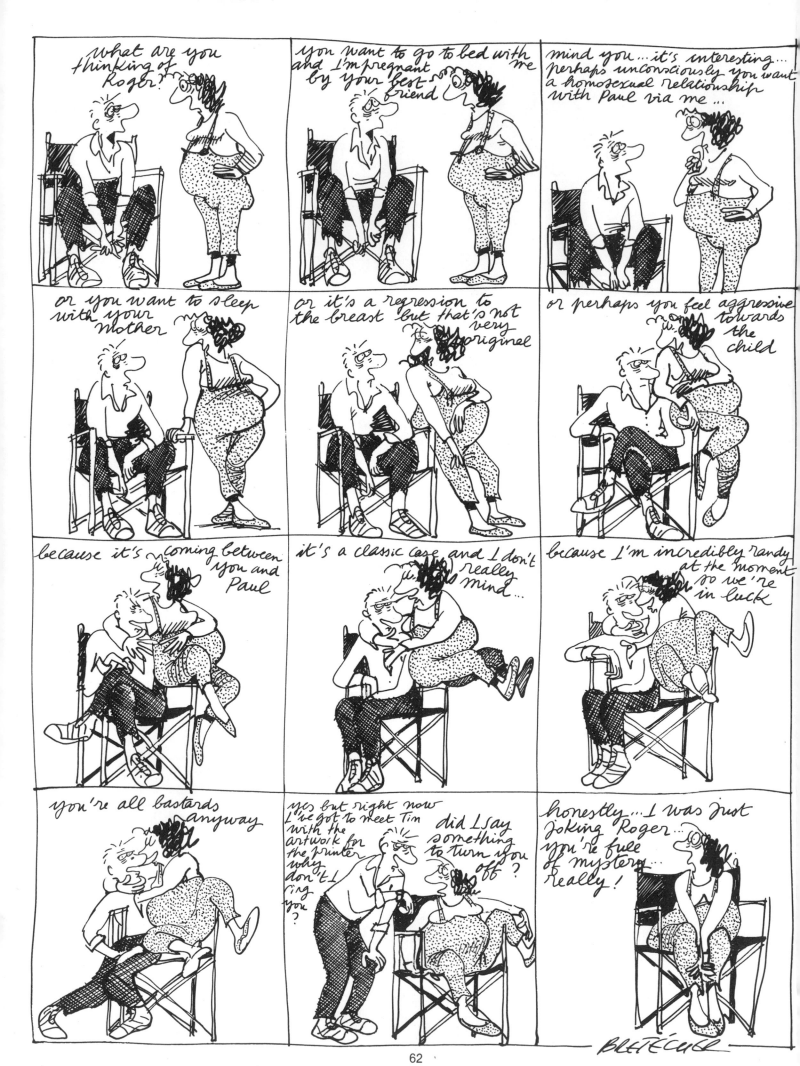

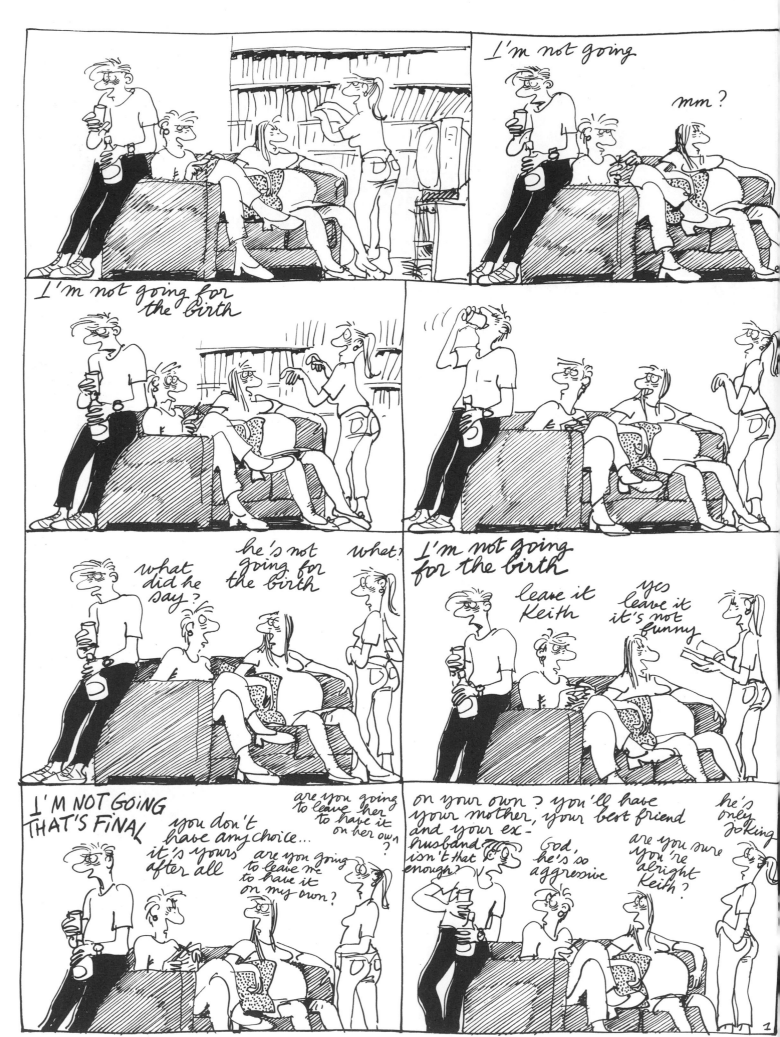